The Selfish Husband

How to Cope with and Transform Your Selfish and Inconsiderate Husband

by Jordan Parker

Table of Contents

Introduction..1

Chapter 1: Reasons Behind His Selfishness 7

Chapter 2: Starting the Changing Process 13

Chapter 3: Activities as a Couple 21

Chapter 4: Defeating the Orange-Eyed Monster 27

Chapter 5: How to Cope Until the Selfishness
Disappears 33

Chapter 6: Make Sure He Keeps Moving Forward..39

Conclusion..43

Introduction

Do you remember your wedding day? How everything felt so perfect, how your heart fluttered when you looked at your husband-to-be, and how you thought that this is the start of your happily-ever-after together?

But looking at your life now... Is it less than everything that you wanted it to be?

Wedded bliss can only go so far, and as the years pass by, your marriage can settle into a comfortable, if not somewhat predictable, routine. However, one of the problems with this is that over time, it's natural that your husband may become more focused on his own needs and desires, and less focused on yours. Gone is the man who would go out of his way to make your feel special, from waking you up with breakfast in bed in the morning, to picking you up after work so that you won't have to endure the trip home alone. After a few years into your marriage, you can consider yourself lucky if you get a good morning kiss when you wake up, let alone a breakfast tray in bed.

A selfish husband can be defined in many ways, ranging from a husband who would rather stay out with his friends than stay home with you, to a husband who watches television all day and does not lift a finger to help out with household chores. However, even husbands who work instead of loaf around can be considered selfish, if he places a lot more attention and importance to his job over your well-being and your marriage.

Having a selfish husband can cause a lot of friction and stress within a relationship. It can cause negative emotions such as anger, frustration, disappointment, and resentment; and as time goes on, these negative emotions become deeper. They start to permeate into the marriage, and often times, you'll start to find fault with everything he does, and can be quick to become angry with your spouse. What's more, a selfish husband doesn't only affect your marriage, but it can also affect you as an individual, and the course of your own life and daily experiences. How unfair is that?

You may start to wonder what caused this change in your husband, and you may also start doubting why you are unable to make him change this negative behavior.

Of course, there's also another side of the coin: you may have entered into this marriage full knowing that your husband has selfish tendencies. When you got married, you may have had this romantic notion that you could change your husband and his selfish ways, or that over time he would care about you more and more.

In any case, I'm sure you're wondering: It actually possible to change your husband, or help him see that his selfish ways are destructive and unnecessary?

The answer is "Yes," although it can sometimes be a long process, depending on the stubbornness of your husband's personality. It's possible that the more you try to force your husband to change, or nag at him or rag on him, the more likely he will resist. You will both end up frustrated with each other, and additional negative feelings will bloom. So instead, I urge you to read this book and follow the strategic guidelines set forth to consequently make him a willing and cooperative party in his own transformation.

Let's get started!

Chapter 1: Reasons Behind His Selfishness

To be able to start the transformative process in your husband, the first thing that you have to understand is the reason why he is selfish to begin with. If you entered your marriage with your husband already having a selfish attitude, it is still possible to help him start the transformative process if you try and understand why he had a selfish attitude growing up. Was he the type of child that was spoiled by his parents? Was he the type of child who felt entitled? If you and your husband have a very open relationship, and if he is good at communication, you can simply talk to your husband about this problem. He may openly admit to being selfish, and let you know outright that he can't help it – that's just who he is. Many introspective men realize their own flaws and can admit them openly, but without a willingness to do anything about it. If this describes your husband, then consider yourself one step ahead of the game.

However, it is more likely that your husband might feel attacked, offended, and defensive by your line of questioning. It might be easier to talk to other people who have been close to your husband while he was growing up, for example his parents, his siblings, or his childhood friends. What's more, you are more likely to get a straight, honest, and complete answer from these people, especially if they know that you are trying to help your husband and your relationship.

If your husband's selfish attitude is a more of a recent development, it is most likely caused by external influences. First, take a look at your home. Has something changed in your home? Are there more bills to pay? Is there less money coming into the household? When circumstances around the home change, and for the worse in terms of finances, it's possible that your husband's behavior has changed as a defensive mechanism.

If you feel that nothing has changed in your home life, the next thing that you can look at is your husband's work environment. Is there something about work that's bothering him, such an overly-demanding boss, or a co-worker that he can't stand? These factors could also be causing a negative reaction in your husband, and his selfish behavior could be a way to cope with them.

Finally, look at your husband's friends. Although he's a grown man and mature adult, you need to realize that he is not immune to peer-pressure, and if there is a friend whom your husband wants to impress, he could be acting more macho and selfish to establish his dominance as a man in the household. The good thing about these external factors is that they are most likely temporary, and even if they last for a long time, your husband may be able to adjust and return to normal, or at least strike a balance. If he's having trouble adjusting, you may need to get creative to help find a more positive, constructive solution. For example, what about a compromise where you suggest that he invites his buddies over to watch the weekly football game on your big screen TV in the living room, and you make snacks and bring them all beer, but without sticking around to watch the game with them. That's a small price to pay for him to feel macho, and then when the guys leave, he'll likely be more loving and thankful to have such a cool wife so he can show off to his friends that he's the man of the house, even if just for this single pre-arranged agreement.

That being said, you need to keep yourself as a priority as well, and draw a line. There's a limit as to where you can and will indulge your husband and his negative behavior, and perhaps even understand his situation. The line you establish should never compromise your own self-respect, or the respect that you demand your husband has for you, and shows to you even in front of his friends. If your husband sees that you are willing to lie down and act as a human doormat, there's a MUCH smaller chance that he will undergo the difficult process of changing his selfish ways. Draw a line that you feel comfortable with (and yet one that is fair and giving to him as well), then stick to it, and if he crosses that line, you better be prepared to put your foot down. Tell him that there will be consequences, and be prepared to act them out.

Chapter 2: Starting the Changing Process

Once you have figured out what is causing the selfish behavior in your husband, whether it is an internal or an external cause, you can go about creating a strategy on how to help change your husband's negative attitude. If you find that your husband's source of selfish behavior is internal, don't be surprised if his attitude is harder to change. Society has unfortunately often taught men that women are an object of their pleasure and purpose, and that men are somehow socially, physically, and emotionally superior to them. Of course as women, we know this isn't true. It's merely another kind of societal discrimination. But unfortunately, it's true that many men are a product of this kind of thinking, and it can be very hard to change their outlook towards women.

Talking with your husband is the first step to trying to change his attitude, especially if it stems from a lifetime of being selfish. It may surprise you how many of your marital problems can be solved just by simply talking to your husband and airing out your grievances towards him. There are many men who are actually unaware of their selfish behavior and its negative consequences, simply because it's the way they have been acting their whole lives and no one has told them otherwise. If this is the case, consider yourself lucky, because your husband will most likely be willing to listen to you, and be willing to put an effort towards changing his attitude. However, don't be frustrated when he falls back into his old patterns every now and again, because it's not easy to change a personality trait that your husband has had his entire life without occasional setbacks. The best way to ensure that your husband does not forget is by positive reinforcement: simply by paying a compliment and saying thank you shows that you appreciate the effort that he is putting into his transformation. It will also help boost his willingness to change more.

However, if you find that the source of his selfishness has deeper roots, it could be time to create a power-strategy. For this, you will need to overcome your own emotions and frustrations, and think of your husband's problem from a cold business-like mindset. Think of it like a problem that you need to tackle, or a task that you need to do, without any emotional attachment.

It's best to start by having a serious talk with your husband. But it needs to be a strategically planned talk where you calmly touch on certain points in a way that won't trigger any of his defense mechanisms. The best way to initiate such a discussion is by scheduling it in advance, and setting a time limit for how long it will take. Let him know that there's something important you want to talk to him about, tell him what the general topic is, and let him know the anticipated timeframe (i.e.: "it will take no longer than half an hour"). Then politely *ask* him when he is available for such a discussion. Of course since you want him to start changing instantly, you might be hoping that he says "Sure honey, let's sit down and talk now." But most likely, since he will want to avoid such a discussion, or at least delay it because he feels it will be all about pointing out his flaw, he may choose to postpone it for a few days. Be respectful of his desire to wait a day or two – if that's what he wants – and both agree on a date and time to have the discussion. If the two of you often fight or have emotionally charged arguments, you may even want to let him know that your intention is not for this to be a fight or an argument, but that you want to have a very calm talk to brainstorm about how to improve your relationship. The benefit of scheduling in advance is that you will both have time to reflect on the topic, and enter the conversation from a calm position, versus taking him by surprise and triggering his immediate defensiveness.

During the actual talk, it's possible that he may still become defensive about the topic, so I'll give you some pointers in a bit that will help you with this. But try to keep the discussion on topic. Avoid discussing any other of his flaws, except his selfishness. If he wants to start discussing your flaws to even out the playing field, then offer to schedule another discussion the following day to talk about those, but that this particular discussion's topic is about his selfishness.

Be careful not to speak down to him, or talk in a way to implies you have the upper hand, or are the better person. Being condescending will hurt, not help, your ultimate goal. Try to merely express your thoughts and problems in a safe, controlled environment, in a calm way when you are alone. While you and your husband love and trust each other, there is no discounting that when tempers are running high, hurtful words, or worse, physical violence, can occur. If you and your husband have agreed to talk on a predetermined time and place, you are in an environment where things are less likely to get out of hand. Second, this talk will help you find a clear and level head while you discuss your problems with your husband, even if emotions arise every now and again. Being calm and collected during this situation allows both you and your husband to offer constructive criticism to each other, and find possible solutions to your problems together. Finally, you and your husband may be able to find a way to communicate thoughts, emotions, and worries that you have never shared with each other, simply because you are given this kind of environment to work in.

It is possible that suggesting a serious spousal talk, even in a calm way, may make your husband defensive and angry. No one likes being reminded that they are not playing their part, and knowing that you feel strongly enough about this issue to have "a talk" can make a husband feel inadequate and unwilling. Nonetheless, it is important that you are honest with your feelings, and that you are ready to calmly deal with any defensive or negative response from your husband. Also be prepared to remind him that you love him, and that you are his friend not his enemy. Let him know you married him because you wanted to work with him (not against him) through the good and the bad, and that this is simply just one little kink in the road, and you want to iron it out before it gets too big. You need to work hard to remain calm, mature, and loving throughout this process. Yes, I know it may be hard, but if you want to transform your husband instead of just fighting with him, then I assure you: This is the only way.

Be open and honest about your concerns and observances, and the goals that you want to achieve by sitting down and talking earnestly. If your husband insists that this is a problem that will go away on its own and that he doesn't want to discuss it, you can consider suggesting a compromise. For example, tell your husband that you can leave your situation as it is for a while (say, a month or two) without discussing it, but if you feel or see that there is no progress, then you must talk openly and honestly as spouses. If he still insists that a serious talk is not necessary, tell him that this is exactly the kind of behavior which makes it necessary in the first place, and that you insist on working through it together. Remind him again that you are his friend and that you love him dearly, but that you require communication even if it isn't always something he wants to discuss.

Before your talk, take some time apart to reflect and write down all the problems that you want to talk to your husband about, with specific examples of times when you feel he has been unjustifiably selfish. Write down not only the incidences, but also how they made you feel, and any consequence they had on you. Writing them down beforehand will make it easier for you to organize your thoughts, and make sure that you haven't forgotten anything important. You can also write down the goals that you want to achieve during and after your self-counseling sessions, so that you can also see if you are achieving what you set out to do in the first place. If you want to set specific goals instead of general goals, this may prove beneficial. For example, instead of saying "I want you to help out more with household chores," say something like "I would like you to do the dishes at least 3 days a week after dinner, so that I don't have to cook dinner and then do the dishes afterwards every single night."

Another option to this "talk" is to do it with the help of an impartial third-party marriage counselor. That way, you will have an unbiased perspective of an outsider who has experience helping couples through tough times, and getting them to see the other person's perspective. Some men immediately disregard this as an option, not wanting to air their grievances to an outsider. But on the other hand, some men actually feel more comfortable in this position, because they want to avoid simply being attacked by their wife who they feel is being unreasonable. It may take a third party to explain the consequences of their selfish behavior on you, rather than you explaining it yourself, for your husband to actually see the light. Going to a marriage counselor's office for the first time can be intimidating, and a lot of couples choose to avoid doing so because of the stigma that is attached. But truly, it may be just what you need, especially if "the talk" didn't go as planned. In this case, take a deep breath, take your husband's hand as his friend and lover, and take that first step towards a better relationship.

Chapter 3: Activities as a Couple

One of the things that marriage counselors often recommend is that you spend more time together as a couple, and do more fun activities together. It's a great way to remind couples of their importance to each other, and the fun that can be had together, as well as a way to strengthen the existing bond between them. There are three types of activities that you can choose from as a couple: intimate, non-intimate, and social. Try to engage in all three types.

These activities are designed to help your husband open up emotionally towards you more, so that there is an easier flow when it comes to the communication between the two of you, and so that he can begin to see you as a friend again, and not as an enemy. This allows your husband to become less emotionally guarded, so that talking about your problems as a couple becomes easier.

1. Intimate and sexual

Of course, the most important activities that a couple can share together are intimate activities. After all, these are activities that you are supposed to do with your spouse, and only your spouse. However, it's not just having sex that couples can share when it comes to intimate activities. Ask your husband to join you in the shower, or give your husband a surprise full-body massage with essential oils when he comes home from work. If you're looking for inspiration, think like a love-struck teenager! If you were a love-struck teenager, what would you do to make those butterflies flutter in your tummy? If you have the time and the money, plan a weekend getaway to a nearby countryside. Book a bed and breakfast together, and spend that weekend reconnecting and getting to know each other again. This will also give you time to talk about your problems.

2. Intimate, but non-sexual

Spending time with your spouse in a non-sexual but intimate setting can be just as important as spending time together making love and engaging in other sexual activities. Even simple things such as cooking meals or cleaning the house together can become intimate activities when you have the right mind-set for them (and good background music). Changing your home environment can be essential to helping your husband transform his life. Why not do some DIY projects together, such as painting the rooms of your home, or perhaps creating a scrapbook together of your most memorable moments together.

Or why not get away from your day-to-day life altogether and spend a weekend camping or hiking? The change of scenery, the fresh air, and the solitude of the wilderness can be just what your relationship needs to get back on track.

3. Social

It is also important to spend time with your friends as a couple, so that your routine is as normal as possible. Spending time with your friends and loved ones will also give your husband a chance to take a break from focusing on solving your problems, thus "recharging" him and getting him ready to tackle those issues again.

It will also give you a chance to observe your spouse in a setting where there are other people around. Does he change his attitude? Is he suddenly more attentive and considerate of your needs? If his selfish behavior suddenly disappears when you are in the company of other people, it may mean that you have a deeper, more serious problem than you originally thought. This will be discussed further in the following chapter.

The key to finding activities that can help and sustain you as couple is variety. Try to find different activities each time you go out together, or otherwise find a way to spice up activities that you know you enjoy together as a couple.

Chapter 4: Defeating the Orange-Eyed Monster

Most people associate colors with certain emotions, such as red for anger or love, yellow for cowardice, blue for calmness, and black for sadness. Orange can be associated with greed and avarice, so if a jealous person is said to be possessed by the green-eyed monster, a person who is selfish can be said to have an orange-eyed monster.

It is one thing for your spouse to act selfish and disinterested all the time, whether you're home alone together, or with other people, but it is a completely different situation when your spouse acts differently when you are alone, and when you are with friends. If your spouse suddenly becomes considerate and empathetic if and only if you're with other people, but reverts back to his selfish ways the minute you come home and are alone again, then you have a deeper and more alarming problem. His changing attitude means that your husband is aware of his selfishness, but does not care about you enough to change his ways. However, he does care about public opinion of him, which is why he presents a completely different front when you are around other people.

If you are living in this kind of situation, it is a very difficult problem for which to find a solution. You have two choices: to try and change your husband immediately, or get out of the marriage as soon as you can. This time, there can be no middle ground, no probation period where you will see if your husband will change. He has probably been aware of his actions and their consequences for a long time, and he just does not care about the negative consequences that they have on you. The important thing here is to be able to pick and stick to one decision. If you choose to leave your marriage, make sure that you stand by your choice, even if your ex-husband comes back to you on bended knees, pleading for another chance. You will probably hear a lot of promises about him being able to change, and how he won't be able to survive without you. However, keep in mind that this man is only doing this now when you're gone from his life, which means that he wasn't able to appreciate you while you were around. There's something to be said about that old cliché about the leopard and his spots, after all. This choice is a drastic and life-changing one, and should only be considered if you feel that there is no chance of your husband changing his selfish attitude.

On the other hand, if your husband says that he is willing to change and put an effort to transform his selfish attitude, by all means, give him a chance. Sometimes people just need to know that someone has faith in them to be able to do things that they never thought they would be able to do. You may have to point out his selfishness frequently, letting him know that you are a human too, and asking how he would like it if the situation were reversed. If you can learn to do this calmly and matter-of-factly, without being emotionally charged, it will be more effective. And again, try your best not to be condescending, even though it may sometimes feel like you're trying to teach a little child a very obvious lesson about the Golden Rule (to treat others as you would like to be treated).

One of the things you can do to help remove that orange-eyed monster from your husband is to nurture his giving side. This may be difficult to do, especially if you are feeling frustrated and fed up with his selfish behavior. But again, you need to be calm, mature, smarter, and more strategic. Simply put, nagging and criticizing often doesn't work, so try something different. Look for something that your husband can take care of, and put time and effort into nurturing. If your husband likes animals, look for something small that he can take care of, such as a puppy or a guinea pig. Seeing how much an animal can flourish under his care can help your husband transform his selfish attitude towards others. If your husband is not too keen on animals, encourage him to take up gardening, or get him an interesting-looking house plant or indoor herb pot. Not only can he nurture his caring side when he grows and take care of plants, studies have also shown that gardening is a great way to relieve stress.

Last, you should realize that men are often more sensitive and receptive than they let on, and for the same reason that speaking to them negatively puts them off so much, speaking to them positively can make them really happy. By way of positive reinforcement, for example thanking him and giving a big hug or kiss when he doesn't something nice for you, it will reinforce the concept that you really like it when he is giving, and that he will be rewarded for it. It sounds elementary, yes, as if you are teaching a dog a new trick by giving it a treat every time it does something right, but hey, there's a reason that's how dogs are trained. It works. Don't be too over the top that he figures out what you're up to though. Try to keep the rewards and kind words subtle enough that they will be effective, yet not appear on his conscious radar.

Helping your husband transform his attitude can be a very difficult task, especially if the selfish attitude is deeply entrenched into his personality. However, with patience, determination, and a little bit of strategy, you can defeat this particular problem altogether.

Chapter 5: How to Cope Until the Selfishness Disappears

The only way that you can keep your sanity during this whole process is to make sure that you also have time for yourself. And I mean, yourself alone. Your husband will not appreciate you breathing down his neck, watching his progress every step of the way, and sooner or later, you will get tired acting like a hall monitor as well. Find time for yourself, and focus on three areas of your wellbeing: your physical side, your emotional side, and your mental side.

THE PHYSICAL SIDE

There's something to be said about physical exercise, whether you're running cross-country, hitting the gym, or even doing housework. Not only does it give you an outlet to release your frustration and negativity, it also distracts you from the problems that you and your husband are having. What's more, exercise releases endorphins in your body, and endorphins are known as "happy hormones." They are the same hormones that are released from your brain after sex, or after eating really good chocolate. They make you feel happy, contented, and relaxed.

It doesn't matter what kind of physical activity you do, as long as you find something that you enjoy. If you're really in need for an activity that will help you get through this trying time, look for something that can pump up your adrenaline just a little bit. You don't have to do something as extreme as skydiving or base jumping. Go get some friends and go on a long drive while blasting 80s music! Visit the nearest tourist attraction, spend a weekend at a bed and breakfast in the country, or maybe even go to the nearest theme park and ride a roller coaster or two. This will also be the time for you to pamper yourself and indulge just a little bit. Go and treat yourself to a spa day at that new spa you've been eyeing.

Finding new experiences that will bring you a rush of excitement and just a little bit of thrill or calmness can be just what you need to get all that frustration and anger towards your situation out of your system.

THE EMOTIONAL SIDE

Emotional scarring can and does last deeper and longer than physical scarring. Hurtful words can leave a lasting impression that you won't forget, and you can bet that something you may have said in anger has probably stuck in your husband's mind as well.

There's a line from a song that goes, "Even lovers need a holiday, far away, from each other". During this trying and emotional time, you and your husband may find yourselves at odds every now and again. To help yourself stay on course, find something to do that makes you feel good. Remember that you are an individual, and entirely self-sufficient. Go shopping, grab some drinks with friends, or curl up in bed with a good book and a mug of hot apple cider. There's bound to be something that's your "go-to" comfort move: Do it!

However, being emotionally stable doesn't always mean going after things that are pleasurable. You may also want to consider visiting a psychiatrist for yourself to be able to talk about your problems and your emotions in a safe place. It may help you get through your own issues by talking to your psychiatrist one-on-one, as there might be issues you won't be able to talk about with your husband at your side. You may find a way to become a more resilient person on your own, such that your husband's flaws tend to bother you less and you can just easily brush them off. Not that his flaws should be excused, but you should always be looking to self-improve, no matter what your situation in life.

There is a disclaimer, however. Make sure that your "go-to" move isn't something that will cause further strain to your relationship with your husband. In the interest of full disclosure, you may also want to let your husband know that you are seeing a psychiatrist on your own.

THE MENTAL SIDE

There will be many times during this whole period where your brain just feels so full that it feels like it's going to explode with just a little push. It's not enough to keep yourself physically active and emotionally satisfied; you should also find ways to keep yourself mentally stimulated.

Being mentally stimulated is an experience that has numerous benefits for you and your relationship with your husband. Not only will you find another effective outlet to decrease your negative emotions, you may also be able to find new activities for you to explore as a couple.

What are some good ways for mental stimulation? Here are just a few ideas:

- Visit a new place that you've always wanted to go, but never been to before. It's a complete experience: you will get your physical activity from exploring around, your mental stimulation from meeting new people, seeing new sights, and eating new food, and the experience will give you an emotional satisfaction that is hard to equal.

- Read a good stimulating book, or a newspaper to learn about current world events.

- Try "brain training" – it's the latest trend that works your brain the same way going to the gym works your muscles. And the best part? It's typically done in the form of fun games that you can play on your iPhone or iPad! The results are proven to improve your memory and attention.

Chapter 6: Make Sure He Keeps Moving Forward

Perhaps the most difficult aspect during this whole process is making sure that you and your husband do not revert back to your old habits. You and your husband are, after all, human, and it's hard not to go back to something familiar. So you'll have to remain vigilant to avoid him becoming selfish again, and you becoming a resentful nag.

The first step is identifying what kind of behaviors or actions trigger the selfish side of your husband. Isolate these triggers, and see what you can change, especially if some of them can be found in your marriage or in your household. If they are otherwise unchangeable, make sure that you and your husband avoid them as much as possible. For example, if a stressful day at work tends to trigger his selfishness (and lack of motivation to help with cleaning the dishes later), then you can together create a system whereby he texts you no later than 4pm to let you know his day was stressful, and then instead of cooking dinner, you can order take-out or delivery. That way, there's no chance that his unwillingness to do the dishes will get under your skin – there will be no dishes to do! The trick is to be creative with your solutions, and try to agree on them as a team. My rule of thumb is this: There are always at least 3 solutions to every problem. Together, you need to brainstorm until you come up with them and choose the best one or one that works for you both.

The second step is identifying what measures are effective in helping your husband transform his behavior. Are your self-counseling "talks" working? Or is it more effective to see a marriage counselor together? Or is it most effective to see therapists on your own? Do you feel closer to each other after doing activities together, or is it better when you do your own thing, then see each other afterward? Effective measures are dependent on the couple, and what may be effective for one couple may not be as effective for another. Keep in mind that it may be difficult to see progress at first, so don't give up if you or your husband feels that there is nothing changing in your relationship.

The third and most important step is acknowledging that change is important, and that it is your determination that will be the deciding factor in this process. How much do you want your husband to transform his selfish attitude? How much does he want to change his attitude? How hard are you both willing to work as a couple and as individuals to be able to achieve this goal? When you find the answers to these questions, you will be able to see whether or not you are ready to take on the challenge of helping your husband transform his selfish attitude. It will take willingness to make an effort on both of your parts, and you may need to accept the fact that you, alone, will need to initiate the effort and try to rev-up his level of willingness.

Conclusion

Having a happy and perfect marriage, like the one you envisioned on your wedding day, is not easy. As a child, you probably read fairytales and wished that you could find your own Prince Charming and live out that happy story-book ending. What you probably never saw, however, was Beauty and the Beast getting marriage counseling because of Beast's anger issues, or Snow White leaving Prince Charming because of his kinky desire to kiss every corpse he came across in the middle of the forest. Fairytale endings do exist, but not in the way that fairytales tout them to be. Reality is different, and we women sometimes need to just grow up and accept that fact.

Marriage is a process and a job: one where both you and your spouse need to learn and grow to be able to make it successful. It's also a process where you have to grow as a couple, as well as individuals. Furthermore, you need to remember to keep it light-hearted and fun a lot of the time, so as to remind each other why you got married in the first place.

Selfishness in marriage is actually a pretty common thing, and sometimes, it can even be a good thing. There might be times when your husband is selfish with his time, but if he's pouring it all into his job because he wants to be able to provide you with a better life, you have to understand that his heart is in the right place, if not completely his ability to balance what is important in life. Furthermore, having a certain degree of selfishness is normal as an individual that is self-reliant and self-sufficient. Maybe you need to just be a little more selfish too, that way you won't have to count on him to take care of you as much. This is called resilience and self-reliance, and it's actually not so bad.

Remember the key to this whole process: Calm Communication! Every step of this whole process will only go forward if you and your husband are open and honest in your communication with each other, in a calm and mature manner, as well as other people who may be helping you through the whole process. From the moment that you tell your husband about his selfish attitude, and how you wish to help it change for the better, you need to be able to establish an open line of communication where you both feel safe and unattacked.

It may not be easy, and it may not be quick, and there may be times when you feel like you've hit a wall, or days when you feel like you're taking one step forward and two steps back. But don't give up! Take a deep breath and keep on moving forward, and one day, you'll wake up next to the man you've helped transform into a more empathic, giving, loving husband.

Thanks for purchasing this book, and I really hope you found it helpful. If you did, please take a moment to leave a review on Amazon – that would be much appreciated!

Made in the USA
Monee, IL
07 January 2021